THE
GOD TRIBE
OF
SHABAZZ
The True History

By
ELIJAH MUHAMMAD
Messenger of Allah

**Compiled & Edited by
Minister Nasir Makr Hakim**

Published by
Secretarius MEMPS Publications
111 E Dunlap Ave, Ste 1-217
Phoenix, AZ 8502-78020
Phone & Fax (602) 466-7347
Email: secmemps@gmail.com
www.memps.com

Write for Free Catalog!

THE GOD TRIBE OF SHABAZZ

Copyright © 2012
Secretarius MEMPS Publications

All rights reserved.
No part of this book may be reproduced
in any form, except for the
inclusion of brief quotations in
reviews, without permission
in writing from the author/publisher.

ISBN-13: 978-1475026450
ISBN-10: 1-475026-45-5

PRINTED IN THE UNITED STATES OF AMERICA

Introduction

Table of Contents

Introduction v
KNOWLEDGE OF HISTORY IS KEY............................... 1
UNDERSTANDING THE KNOWLDEGE OF SELF 7
ORIGINAL MAN EXPERIMENTS ON SELF 11
THOUGHT AND MANIFESTATION................................ 15
THE WHOLE TRIBE OF SHABAZZ 17
THE TRIBE AFTER THE BLAST 23
THE POWER OF THOUGH IN THE MIND 27
THE WILL WHICH TRANSCENDS TIME 31
THE MOON GOD 35
UNIVERSAL CHANGE BY DESIGN 45
SHABAZZ, THE SCIENTIST IN PERSPECTIVE............. 49
ORIGINAL TRIBE FROM SPIRIT OR PHYSICAL MAN? .. 53
THE TRIBE OF SHABAZZ IN EAST ASIA (AFRICA) 59
JOHN HAWKINS AND THE MAKING OF A SLAVE 61
ABRAHAM IS NOT YOUR FATHER 75
BEING ASHAMED OF SALVATION 79
THE PROPHESY OF ABRAHAM 83
   East, West & Red Indians... 83
A LOST AND FOUND NATION 87
THE LAKE OF FIRE 91
THE NEW QUIBLAH 97
WHY DID ALLAH MAKE DEVIL? 99
THE NEW WORLD WON'T ACCEPT THE OLD 105
THE GREAT BOOK 109
Catalog Requests 115

Introduction

The history of the God Tribe of Shabazz is one of the most elusive subjects of the Supreme Wisdom as taught by Messenger Elijah Muhammad, partly because it is spread out over so much time, on so many lectures and in so many different articles.

While mining through various audio lectures by the Messenger, I came across one over the Saviour's Day weekend. After listening to it with great joy, Allah, Master Fard Muhammad, put it on my heart to do the research, mining and compilation to share this most profound revelation with those who have ears.

To that end, this book is presented to share just how thankful we, the Blackman and woman of America, should be, to be so loved that our God, Master Fard Muhammad, Allah in person, has appeared among us to return us to our own kind.

I must confess, I was just overwhelmed at the affect this revelation had on me, because regardless to how much of the teaching you may have heard, read or experience, when Allah, Master Fard Muhammad blesses you to see, you SEE. I am not going to put much time into describing the emotion or mindset of what one goes through when Allah allows you to see, but what I will share is that you would have to be a believer to understand.

The Tribe of Shabazz is not simply the offspring of a group of people who were the product of a disgruntled scientist who went into Africa to prove that He could "make a people that could withstand anything," but a continuum of a vein of expression characteristic of how we as black people, who, when in our natural mind did things that were still superior to the best minds of mankind today. We are so far from what is actually natural for the Blackman, that we think that the little chance happenings of this civilization today are brilliant; when in fact, the incidental actions of the Original Blackman is

Introduction

considered SUPERNATUAL by today's standards.

The Messenger of Allah, Elijah Muhammad, delves so far into the most profound depths of wisdom when sharing with us what our God, in person, Master Fard Muhammad, had revealed, it makes you wonder about who is out there dormant and simply waiting to hear that particular word, sentence, paragraph or perspective that will make the light in or above their heads illuminate with Allah's voice communicating with them. In other words, it's not necessary to be mining Facebook, Twitter or Google+, etc, for revelation. It's being handed to you here.

This Supreme Wisdom is not cheap. Why waste any time convincing those who are dead centered on disbelieving. If anyone can change their hearts, it would be by Allah's grace. It's not your job to force belief.

You can lead a horse to water... but who wants to (dah)? It's too late in the day. Allah and his Messenger only want willing souls at this point; so do we.

It would be premature to ask you to reclaim something of which you have no knowledge. Therefore, after you read this book and if you are blessed with the spirit of inspiration and a willingness to be enlightened, you can enroll to learn more as a student.

Minister Nasir Hakim
Founder, Messenger Elijah Muhammad Propagation Society

Introduction

THE GOD TRIBE OF SHABAZZ

KNOWLEDGE OF HISTORY IS KEY

Allah, God Almighty, in the person of Master Fard Muhammad, has revealed to us and has given to me the understanding of [a] particular teaching that I am now teaching you and others. [It is to teach you] how to understand it and how to understand the history of the prophets and their sayings as recorded in the Bible and Holy Quran. He has given me this understanding and He has revealed [the] secrets to me. As it [was] written, that God always reveals His aims or His secrets only to prophets or servants whom He chooses. I don't represent myself as a prophet, because you don't need a prophet today. The time that we are living in today is the end of the prophets. There is no need for a prophet after the coming of God. There's no need for a prophet at the present world's time. The prophets were before and were sent throughout the 6,000 years of the Caucasian's history on our planet. There were 3 great ones: namely

THE GOD TRIBE OF SHABAZZ

Yakub, the father of the Caucasian race; Moses, Jesus and Muhammad the last.

Muhammad takes up in the resurrection. Muhammad in the 7th century, after Jesus, gave us a picture of what we may expect after 1400 years or 1400 years after his death. He gave us that or rather Allah revealed it to him and we have it here in the Qur'an. This Qur'an teaches just what we may expect today. It leads us up to the resurrection of the so-called American Negroes. They are the ones to be resurrected. The entire darker peoples of the earth are in the time of a resurrection for their future, because it's the end of a world that has ruled for the past 6,000 years.

These things that I'm saying are very, very important [for] you [to] hear, and very important [for] you [to] believe. [Likewise, they are] very important that you understand them and [take] them to heart, because as I first said, without the knowledge of history, we are lost; therefore, [we] cannot calculate [anything]. [Like] a man without the knowledge of mathematics, he cannot build. He is subject a civilization who

KNOWLEDGE OF HISTORY IS KEY

understands mathematics. [For] takes mathematics to build a civilization. The knowledge of mathematics is found in the Universe or the Universal order of things and is the beginning [of] the very root in which and upon which the universe is based; it is mathematics. It is the very root of the religion of Almighty God, the religion of peace, Islam, Mathematics. They are the true religion that we have, and it is compared with the true religion of Islam. Mathematics is truth. Islam is true; therefore, the two go together.

I say you must know yourself, as God Almighty has revealed it to me. You must give a listening ear to [the knowledge and history of] yourself.

Let us talk on the history, because it is the thing that we should know. History makes man. Without the knowledge of history, how can we prepare a future for ourselves without the knowledge of history? How can we tell where we're standing at present? History makes us; true history is our God. We must know what was before we can know what is and what is yet to come. This [is what]

THE GOD TRIBE OF SHABAZZ

Almighty God, whose proper name is Allah, came in the person Master Fard Muhammad [to teach us]. We can gladly give praise forever and teach that praise of this glorious One to our children [so] that they may teach it to their children and their children's children throughout the unending years to come.[1]

What I teach is life to them. What I bring them out of is death. My mission is the last of the Scientists, or the truth that is to come to the world before the world is destroyed. You will not have no other Messenger. I am the last one. Behind me comes God Himself. I don't care if I will live through it, but after me God will come or if it pleases Him I may be with Him. If I am not with Him, this is the Last.

This truth brings you into the knowledge of yourself and of God. There is nothing hidden [of] the God to much in this teaching. You learn what God is and learn to be God yourself. This is the Real God's teaching: What is God, how things were made and brought about. This is

---
[1] Tribe of Shabazz, 1962, Audio, EL004

KNOWLEDGE OF HISTORY IS KEY

what it is. This is the last Wisdom to be given to the world and a knowledge of how this world was made.[2]

---

[2] Buzz Anderson Interview, Phoenix AZ, 1964.

6 THE GOD TRIBE OF SHABAZZ

UNDERSTANDING THE KNOWLDEGE OF SELF

We have never had the knowledge of ourselves since we were brought here for slave purposes. We didn't know anything about ourselves. Our grandparents and our parents many of whom have not heard the ancient history of their people don't know who they are. We say we teach them a knowledge of himself; meaning that he doesn't know himself. The average black person don't know himself, because he cannot give any history of himself beyond the time he was put in the cotton field of the South. That history he got from his slave-master. He doesn't know anything beyond that.

This teaching is to give him a knowledge of his fathers and the origin of everything except himself, because you cannot get the origin of himself unless you give him his birth record. You can't give him the origin of himself because you can't give him his birth record.

I asked God was not there a "beginning." We often would wrangle over the beginning. How did the atom of life begin in the universe? That is such a level of wisdom that you are bound to differ from me and I am bound to differ from you. There is no date for it and to say how it came into actuality or activity is too much to discuss.[3]

The first life-germ was capable [aware] with its own intelligence of self to cause what you and I see today to come into existence from nothing. It had no basis. There was no base to create a sun or moon, but He created it Himself by the power of His own intelligence. As we today are fast learning that the intelligence of the scientist can bring into being anything that we can conceive into our brains we can make it a reality. That's the God. You are learning that. The white race is bearing me witness that Man is God. The Whiteman once was as dumb as dumb could be.[4]

---

[3] Ibid.
[4] Messenger Elijah Muhammad, Baltimore 1960, Audio

UNDERSTANDING THE KNOWLDEGE OF SELF

There is nothing impossible so Allah told me. I questioned Him on this. Now, what makes the God so sure that nothing is impossible? Because if we say anything, [whether it's] this or that is impossible, [and] we yet find ourselves within the circle of something, how can it be impossible to produce, take away or to change anything? It can't be impossible, because you may think something is impossible or don't see the possibility existing there somewhere, but God can still say there is no impossibility. Here is the point He takes. Once upon a time nothing existed. You and I couldn't be sitting here discussing this because we came from nothing. So, if we were made out of nothing into something then that does away with the impossible. There can't be the impossible, because here we are ourselves produced out of nothing. That's very beautiful and a good answer.

10 THE GOD TRIBE OF SHABAZZ

ORIGINAL MAN EXPERIMENTS ON SELF

Just like people argue with you about who is God and say that man can't be God. That's a foolish man talking like that. You can't replace man. If man is not God, then try and replace him. You can't replace him, so that's a proof right there that he's God. Your mind doesn't exceed the limitation of the First Man who is God, because He came down through us. We have been experimenting from ourselves.[5]

The true knowledge or science of the world that you and I are living in today was kept back and hidden. It was [kept] a secret among the scientist until the world that you and I have known had lived [out] its time and [fulfilled] the work it was [made] to do. Today it's disappearing and a new world is budding or giving birth in place of an old one.

---
[5] Table Talk of Muhammad, December 1972.

THE GOD TRIBE OF SHABAZZ

We, the so-called American Negroes, [are] members, I repeat, from a Tribe of ours by the name of Shabazz.

We, the Nation of Islam, the Nation of righteous, the Nation of peace, have always experimented among ourselves on this and that. That's why we know we are the greatest and the wisest people in the universe because our study of the life on other planets. We don't find them experimenting among themselves or on their planet as we are; [consequently], we know that we are the wisest people in the sun.

The so-called Negro, the black man, the lost and found member of a great original nation, is the first on our planet. I want you to remember that we are the first on our planet. We are first before our planet. The planet didn't come before us; we were before the planet. I want you to pay good attention. Take notes on what I say. Attack me on the truth of it if you want to, but I don't have time to contend with you here this afternoon in this short time that I am given....

ORIGINAL MAN EXPERIMENTS ON SELF

We were before the earth. We could not claim ourselves as being the Creators of the universe: The Sun, Moon and Star and the earth if we had been birthed or created after the earth or if we came after the earth, then the earth is older than the God who claimed to be master of the Earth. There is so much talk going on today since Almighty God Allah has visited us and revealed to us the truth that is necessary; very much necessary.

I go into the past to bring you up with the truth to the present time, because that is the trouble with my people, they think they are inferior. They think they are something that God doesn't want. They think that their particular knowledge and way of life is like that of all of our people, regardless to what part of earth that they live on. Some think that they are [more] superior in wisdom and in education than any of their kind on the earth. [To] these I say, [you are] mistaken [in what] you are making yourself. It is due to the lack of knowledge of the black man. I want you to know these things Before we go into an argument over, "He is teaching hate or he's teaching black supremacy." I want to give to you the Blackmans' history. You can say that he's inferior, you can say that he's not superior, you can say that he's not the supreme people if you want to; that's up to you, but I will give you his history and I defy you to disprove it.[6]

---

[6] Christianity Versus Islam, Philadelphia, PA, Nov. 7, 1962, Messenger Elijah Muhammad.

THOUGHT AND MANIFESTATION

Everything that we think is necessary. We then can produce it and bring it into reality. If this house is sitting in my mind, but not yet built, I can bring it out of my mind into reality. That's the God.

You can create the image that is in you; that is in your mind once you can conceive out the image of it [or] of what you want. You then can bring it into being. That which you can't create in your mind is something you can't [create] or do. [Yet], that does not mean that it (that which you have not yet conceived of) is not coming in. It may come in your son's mind or your son's son's mind. That same thing which you were trying to get a hold of, it will come up in somebody else [mind]; that is, if it is necessary [or] if it is good.

[A good example is] our Saviour. The people had been wanting someone to conquer this devil for a long time, so [the idea] kept on going from one [mind] to another then finally His father (Allah) produced the thing that was necessary. That is a son that would be wise enough to destroy the devil. He was lucky to have been the father. Wherever there is a line for something, it will be produced.

Just like the devil wanted to learn how to fly, he kept trying some contraptions until he learned how to get up there in something heavier than air and went on to make the air his servant. It was the same thing when he was on the other side of the ocean. He kept on looking over the vast ocean and couldn't see any end to it. He wanted to see where the Sun was going down on the other side of it, so he kept on until he mastered the waves and the storms until he got over there.[7]

---

[7] Table Talks of Muhammad, December 1972.

THE WHOLE TRIBE OF SHABAZZ

We don't have the date of the beginning of His civilization or whereabouts, because once upon a time the moon and the earth were together. There cannot be a specific spot pointed out where the original building of civilization took place. We do know, according to the teachings of Almighty God to me, that once upon a time we had nothing in the universe but the Sun. After that Stars were made and from stars to stars to stars and stars. They saw that the Star was essential to our well being and from that we began to make Planets. Between the creation of the Sun and the Earth is six trillion years. [The universe] is often referred to as having been made or created in three stages or three divisions: two trillion years to each.[8]

You must know yourself. You can't go and live in the midst of your people on the planet earth nowhere unless you first

---

[8] Buzz Anderson Interviews Messenger Elijah Muhammad, Phoenix, AZ, 1964.

have a knowledge of yourself. I am here with that knowledge for you if you will just accept it. Let's see who we are.

We were brought here in America 400 years ago, according to the history of our enslavement, by Christian White people. I want you to remember they were Christians, not sinners; they were Christians who made our fathers slaves. And it was Christians who did not allow our fathers to become Christians for 300 years. It was not sinners; it was Christians. What was our history?

Historians, students of history: what was the history our people before entering slavery here in America? Where were they? You say in Africa. How long had they been in Africa? Let's chase the history of our people and see who we are. If you don't know yourself, it's due to the fact you don't know your own history. If you know your own history, you know yourself.

How long had our fathers been in Africa before the Whiteman went there and brought them into the Western Hemisphere as slaves? Where were they

THE WHOLE TRIBE OF SHABAZZ

from before they got into Africa or did they originate there? You are scholars and scientist, why don't you know these things?

If we are a people that are to be respected and not be an outcast of the civilized world, what were our fathers before we ever came to America to come into the realization that we are outcast and unwanted people in the society of nations? Where did we come from and was our fathers anything? God has revealed these things.

Almighty God has said to me that before the Whiteman ever brought from that particular continent, we had been there in that particular continent 50,000 years. He again said to me that, before going there, we were in what we call today Arabia, that whole entire peninsula as they call it. Before the Whiteman came there, that country or peninsula was called Arabia. [Although] they have it divided up into many other states [today], it was called Arabia, meaning the First, or Asia. The continent of Africa at that time was called the Jungles of East Asia. Our people who are there today came from a scientist who wanted to make a people who was capable of withstanding the hot sun and could get along with the beast and other wild animals of the jungle.

He went to the other 24 scientist and pleaded with them to allow him to take his family into the jungles of East Asia to make the people he thought would be capable of withstanding anything of nature. That man was one of the Tribe of Shabazz. We are tracing our own fathers' history.

This man belonging to the Tribe of Shabazz was the father of us from 50,000 years ago up until today. [In other words], for 50,000 years he has acted, or rather he was in the place as a father of us. Before this Tribe of Shabazz produced that man, that scientist, there was a Tribe of Shabazz called the Number One Tribe before our deportation from Moon and that deportation from Moon took place 66 trillion years ago. It was one of the Tribes and the only scientific tribe that escaped that great disaster of the explosion on our planet in those days, who came with this part.

THE WHOLE TRIBE OF SHABAZZ

This part [of our planet] dropped 36,000 miles from the original pocket in which it was in at the time of that explosion. That explosion or blast caused this part to drop 36,000 from that original pocket that she rotated in. The part you see at night called Moon, from the force of the blast, took it 12,000 miles away from the original pocket. The part of the earth that dropped 36,000 from its original pocket found another pocket in which to rotate. [Actually] it never stopped. It was too short of a distance for the planet to slow up its speed of rotation. If it had slowed up, it would have affected the people, but it didn't slow up. The blast made and the drop the planet made due to the blast kept the planet rotating at the same rate of speed. The Sun that causes and compels the earth to rotate on an axis, did not lose any power of attraction on either part. She [Sun] kept both parts moving around in their orbit as this other part [Moon] followed us and it also is attached to the same part that it came from for power to continue rotating; so, it [Moon] rotates in our orbit, or rotates around the same planet it came from.

THE GOD TRIBE OF SHABAZZ

THE TRIBE AFTER THE BLAST

This particular Tribe from which our fathers came, after the Earth was fit after the blast, were the first scientist, "explorers," who explored of earth after that blast or Earth's deportation from the Moon. They found the best spot on our planet earth to make a home. They covered [explored] the entire earth. It was our fathers. We are from that same Tribe. They are the ones who set up history for us. They wrote it and told about it. We have it today in the Holy City Mecca put away in a safe keeping vault where no man is able to get to or attack it, or even look upon it except 12 people. There are only 12 people on our planet today that has the privilege to look into that history and they keep the knowledge within themselves among the 12. The only one today who knows the secret of that book is the 12th One who is acknowledged by the other 11 to be God In Person.

THE GOD TRIBE OF SHABAZZ

That book contains all that had happened among us before we made the Moon. I say we, because it was our fathers who made it. There are ways to prove the truth of it. If you are a scholar, scientist or astronomer, you have a way of proving this.

Before we made this moon, we had Mars turning as our Moon for this Earth. Our Earth at that time was approximately 10,000 miles in diameter and 36,000 in circumference; whereas, today it is approximately 24,896 thousand in circumference with the equator - approximately 25,000 thousand miles and straight through at the equator 7,926 miles.

Before the deportation of Moon the Earth was approximately 10,000 miles straight through it and about 36,000 around at the equator. She has always been egg - shaped when the moon was with the Earth. She has never been a totally round sphere.

It was our fathers who came with our planet and have produced for us today

THE TRIBE AFTER THE BLAST

what we have. The God we have today is from that same father.

I want to bring you into the knowledge of yourself. There is no such thing as a God other than us. It is a grave mistake for you to try producing a God other than Man. We, the Blackman, have been God ever since we had a life germ in the universe and the first life germ in the universe was us. This is from God Himself.[9]

---

[9] Messenger Elijah Muhammad, Baltimore, MD, 1960.

26   THE GOD TRIBE OF SHABAZZ

THE POWER OF THOUGH IN THE MIND

Let me say right here, that Men's wisdom lasts or is Supreme until another one that is more Supreme over his comes about. This is the way the Gods run [operate]. We don't have just one Man's wisdom that extends all the time. It's another one. Your wisdom, for example, making that radio may last for 5 or 6 years until another man learns to make a better one and when he learns to make a better one you still get the credit for being the first one to make the radio, but it has been improved upon. You could come back 100 years from now and you wouldn't know your machine, because so much improvement has been made upon it.

Take for instance those who made the Ford motor car. If Ford would look at his car today he would say he was dumb [by comparison]. Although Ford didn't put all the improvements of the car, he was the founder of the car. So it is with wise men in spiritual work and other sciences that we worship of the God that has made and created. We have Them coming at intervals. When ones wisdom is exhausted another one's picks up and He improves on what you have done.

Like the God that divided our planet: He was wise enough to want to have His word bond 100% and to let every man know He was to speak the same language and think the same thing. This was against nature. The heavens and the earth were not created like that; they vary. [Consequently] he failed and got angry and said that since they won't be like He wants them to be I will destroy myself and them too.

He missed, because the universe is made in such a way by the Creator that you can't destroy it yourself or you can't destroy the people of the Creator. Regardless to your plans, whether like Russia or America that has the deadliest and destructive weapons that have been fashioned by any scientist of war of the past, that can destroy human beings on this earth 3 or 10 times if they wanted to; they can't do it. Regardless to what weapons you may use to destroy all life

THE POWER OF THOUGH IN THE MIND

on the earth, you will fail, because there is someone always sitting back behind the curtain that you don't know, who knows what you know. He knows an enemy that can destroy the enemy that you have fashioned. This is the way it was in the time of the Man who wanted to destroy our planet.

THE GOD TRIBE OF SHABAZZ

THE WILL WHICH TRANSCENDS TIME

The present Moon is 66 trillion years old itself or rather being in the present position it's in. Originally it [was part of the earth], but from an explosion it blew out 12,000 miles from the earth and the earth itself dropped 36, 000 miles out of it original orbit. 66 trillion years ago the water on the moon dropped back upon this part. It is without water due to the explosion. That gave us 3/4ths of our surface because we have the water from that part.

The Original man did that. He was a God or Scientist that brought about the explosion due to His dissatisfaction of not being able to have all the people alike and speaking the same dialect. He got angry because he could not make them speak the same dialect all the way around. Our planet at that time was better than 10,000 miles in diameter. Now it is around 8,000 miles in diameter. He had become vexed with his own wisdom; he was unable to do with

THE GOD TRIBE OF SHABAZZ

the people he wanted to with them. He attempted to destroy us. His aim was not to make a moon or satellite for our planet. At that time, according to the teachings of God to me, we had Mars for our moon. It served as our moon before this Scientist tried to destroy us. Since he was unable to do so, we were lucky to come with this part. The people on that part were destroyed. We were called the aboriginal people and we are the aboriginal people today.

In the 6 trillion years before that time in the Creation of life and water, it was the Blackman. You can't find no history that would give you the birth of the Blackman. He has always been.[10]

---

[10] Buzz Anderson Interview, Phoenix, AZ 1964

THE WILL WHICH TRANSCENDS TIME

[The question was asked, "One of the points the Eastern Muslims remark on is that, the Qur'an says that, "He (Allah) neither begets nor is He begotten." Yet, we know that Allah came out of the family of the Tribe of Shabazz, out of the family of The God, and the God is always produced out of a fairly consistent family. From the ranks of this family, we look for the production of a God so that eventually this family actually begets the God. Knowing the Qur'an is true and that what the wise men wrote they meant, even if we don't have an understanding of it, how do we account for this apparent contradiction?]

Messenger: Well, that has two meanings: There was no Tribe of Shabazz with that first God, brother. There wasn't even a tribe. Tribe means many or the head of many. So in the beginning of the Creation of the Life Germ of man, there was no Tribe. That was One God talking there; the Tribes came later. Just like the space was not full of stars when this was going on, [yet] now it's full. We had no Sun in that time, but now we have one around these live eggs that we call planets. We now have a Sun to keep them warm.[11]

---

[11] Table Talks of Muhammad, December 1972.

THE MOON GOD

Allah (God) lay hold on something (the MOON) to compare with our history. Nothing could be better than the MOON for this comparison since Allah (God) in the Person of Master Fard Muhammad taught me that a Black scientist, bent upon destroying us, blasted that part (Moon) away from our Earth. He was the God of the MOON and his intentions were of evil.

We used to say, and many of us still say, that Yakub was the first God of murder which is true of his race (the white race) that he made. Now, the God who tried to destroy us along with himself, his effort to do so, caused the making of our MOON. The God of the MOON had murder and the destruction of the human family in his mind. He was not successful in doing so. Allah (God) used this history of that God to teach us what is in the mind of this people (the white race).

The MOON according to the teachings of Allah (God) Who came in the Person of

THE GOD TRIBE OF SHABAZZ

Master Fard Muhammad, to Whom Praises are due forever, is a part of this Earth. It is as old as the Earth. It was not the idea of the God, who took the MOON from the Earth to make that a part a satellite for the Earth. His idea was to force his rule upon the people of our planet and force all to speak the same dialect, which he was not able to do. Then he decided to destroy all, including the Earth and himself. He went to work by attempting to drill a tube into the Earth's surface. It must have reached approximately the center of the Earth. Then he filled it with high explosives which we call dynamite. However, it was 30 percent more powerful than the present dynamite. Then he set it off. The explosion blasted away a piece of our then - Earth, which according to the MOON'S diameter is approximately 2,160 miles or about one - third the size of our planet Earth.

After that part that you call MOON was blasted away from this part, to the distance of approximately 12,000 miles, she turned over and emptied the water onto this part which we call Earth, depriving herself of life. Until this day,

THE MOON GOD

the MOON has been devoid of the water of life; unable to produce vegetation, unable to moisten the atmosphere, so that man and beast could live on that part of our Earth called MOON.

In this great explosion the MOON was not blasted far enough to make a complete turn herself while rotating around the Earth. Therefore we never see her other side before she is again entering into the shaded side of our Earth. I hope that you pay good attention to these words. Since the MOON has no water and gravitation from the power of water life, which she had before she was blasted away from her own, (the Earth), she is made subject to the Earth because here is the power of growth because of much water (life) covering the surface of the Earth.

The MOON seems to be begging for her life (water). There is no planet which is worthwhile without the presence of water, since water is the base of life, as the Holy Quran teaches us, that out of water Allah (God) created every life.

THE GOD TRIBE OF SHABAZZ

She lost her life and her children, her beautiful covering of vegetation to adorn her surface. She became an old dried-up piece of Earth. She is bossed by the Earth and not by the SUN. She gets her activity through the Earth because her support is from the Earth.

The whole Earth was not very old when this took place, but very old too. She had gone through the stages of trillions of years herself. She is set out here approximately one - quarter (1/4) million miles for a sign too.

It was not the idea of that God to make a sign for us. He had the wicked idea to destroy us because he could not rule us. He destroyed himself and made for us a sign that serves as a reflection of light from the SUN to keep us in the knowledge of the event and our looking at the marvelous piece of work dying through the mistake of one of the Gods.

Poor old piece of our Earth lying out there in space. We are to carry that dead piece because it is deprived of life. The other part, our Earth, is filled with an abundance of life. We cannot say that we

THE MOON GOD

robbed the MOON of its life. The enemy robbed the MOON of its life (water) and poured it onto this part of the planet Earth. This act of saving the water from the destruction of the MOON was of Allah to show that regardless of what happens to the matter (MOON) the original water of life will be saved.

She is still going on her journey around the Earth seeking her life. With her time of rotation around the Earth seeking her life, with her time of rotation around the Earth and her stages made, she is capable of proving her loss of life with her clinging to the power of Earth's gravitation and since she was the Work and Creation of the Hand of the same God that created her with the Earth, she draws one of the most significant signs that she is one of us. The way she affects our life on Earth is in order to show that she is part of us.

The pouring forth of the life blood of the nation from the womb of the woman every 28 days compares with the rotation of the MOON around our planet. This shows that the accuracy of truth, if understood, by the theologians and scientists, of just the secret of the idea of making and the commanding of the MOON... it is impossible to destroy the life of the Originator of the heavens and the Earth. That life will be cared for. The MOON is placed there as a sign of the failure of the effort of that scientist to destroy the life on the Earth.

The blasting away of MOON by an enemy that robbed the MOON of its life (water) and poured it onto this part of the planet Earth can also be compared to the evil white slave-traders guided by John Hawkins (discussed later), the explorer, to come among us and take us by force and bring us to this part of our Earth among strangers whom our fathers knew not. In so doing they made us to lose all, knowledge of ourselves and our kind like this man or God who in his frenzy to try to force all the people to believe as he believed and to speak the same language with no difference in dialect caused the deportation of the MOON from the Earth. So it is with our enemy today. He wants us all to kneel and bow to his way of life

THE MOON GOD

and if he cannot get us to do so, he wants to be rid of us and our Earth.[12]

Since the Moon's number is 66 trillion years and the white man's number is 66 hundred years from the time of his making to the time of his end, the Revelator of the Bible. Rev. 13:18 says, that his number is "the number of a man." The man is the Black man who brought about the deportation of the moon 66 trillion years ago. He was a God (Black man). We never had any other people on the Earth, other than the Black people until 6,000 years ago, according to the teachings to me of Allah (God) Who came in the Person of Master Fard Muhammad to Whom praises are due forever. All of the races and different colors of people which we have on the planet today, were brought from the grafting and making of the white man by his God, Yakub. Many races have been produced from the four (4) colors, black, brown, yellow and white and the intermixing of these colors. The Earth's population is dominated by their four

---

[12] The Flag of Islam, 1974, pg. 11.

major colors (black, brown. yellow and white).

The number of the white man is truly the same as that of the Black man who caused the deportation of the MOON from the Earth. We can add another six (6) because it was six (6) trillion years between the creation of life out of darkness to the creation of the present day SUN which took 6 trillion years. Therefore, if we would add that figure on to the time of the age of the MOON, we would have three (3) 6's there. But we always have three (3) 6's throughout the whole entire stages of the Earth. It was created in six (6) periods of time according to the Holy Quran which is the most accurate and truthful Book, if understood, in the hands of men of the Earth.

We see then, that Allah used the history of the work of the God of the MOON, sixty-six (66) trillion years ago, to teach us of something of ourselves and of our enemy. Here, we the Black man in America stand as a MOON devoid of wisdom and the knowledge of self and others; and the MOON is devoid of water.

THE MOON GOD

We were robbed by a mastermind man with the purpose in mind to destroying the life of the Black man. That is what he began with. In the history of the making of the white man, Yakub, the maker of the white race, taught his people to destroy the Black babies in the very beginning and this is his ultimate aim (to destroy all the Black people of the Earth). There are other significances to the destruction which took place on our Earth and which caused the MOON to be blasted from the Earth but this that I give here is to show why ALLAH (God) used the MOON to show forth the significance of our history under the white American slave-master. Do not forget that the intention of the two Gods (the God of the MOON and the God of the white man) are the same.[13]

---

[13] Ibid.

THE GOD TRIBE OF SHABAZZ

UNIVERSAL CHANGE BY DESIGN

As previously mentioned, In [the MOON God's] effort to destroy the Blackman, He caused a new world of thought to come in.

He split this one (earth) in two. He had taken one part of it and put it out before our eyes to serve as signs, for this part. He wanted to destroy us, but he couldn't. He wanted his teachings to go like the one that went into Africa and we came from him.

Fifty-thousand years ago, as God taught me, a Blackman disagreed with the eleven scientists; the eleven stuck together and let him go and prove his new God wisdom somewhere else. It was Africa into which he went to prove it, in the jungles of Africa [the jungles of East Asia]. He said he could make a people like himself and would bring [everything] to a naught, because they would be strong, powerful and nothing could defeat them. So the eleven said go and make your man, but don't make him here. So he went into the jungles of Africa fifty thousand years ago, so God taught me, and He showed me the signs that I could recognize today. He pointed out to me one night, two little stars in the Southeastern skies: a blue one and a red one. He said, "It's been fifty thousand years since we have seen these two stars," He said, "When they go away out of the skies from our sight this time, it will be fifty-thousand years before they reappear." Every time they reappear there will be a universal change.

The white man recognizes these things; their scholars and scientists, but they don't talk to you on nothing of the kind. A blue star beside a red one; that means removal of a world that doesn't correspond with the original world.

You say, "Well how many more times is it?" The end is up. The wisdom that this One brought is to bring an end to these kind of workings, [also to] show forth something to come after this man's wisdom. There is no wisdom to come after this that will be able to erase this wisdom, because this wisdom is brought

UNIVERSAL CHANGE BY DESIGN

to you from the root of wisdom from the Originator of the Universe.

You notice that the whole universe is egg shaped. The planets in the universe are also egg shaped. They are not perfectly round spheres. Well, this is leaving a little work for some wise man; that is, that [which] I am not able to perfect, then someone must perfect that thing. This is the way that we look at wisdom. When scholars are arguing with each other, they take one word - most time - they don't take a whole book, one word is sufficient for them to argue on. If that is not perfect, then all right, he challenges you to prove your work - these are scientists. I don't say that I'm one, but I can entertain them.[14]

---

[14] Theology of Time Lecture, Chicago, IL, June 4, 1972.

THE GOD TRIBE OF SHABAZZ

SHABAZZ, THE SCIENTIST IN PERSPECTIVE

Dear Holy Apostle:

Can you put three men in perspective for me: The Scientist who produced the deportation, the Scientist who took us into Africa, and Yakub.

Messenger: These are the histories of three great men. Men who are performing god-like work or God's work in their day and time.

Each of these men did a god-like work, but at the time; for example, when the deportation of the moon had taken place, you had taught us that there was no history of the 12; so there was just One. So, his relation to what could have been or what must have been to God, Allah, means He would have had to be It.

THE GOD TRIBE OF SHABAZZ

In terms of the One 50,000 years ago, he disagreed with the 11 and in doing so was no longer considered a God?

Messenger: No, no, no. He was a God. Look at what He got up down there in the jungle.

What he was relative to the other is the question. My understanding was, and I thought you had said that once he left the other 11, the work he did and what he was to do, did not really allow us to call him one of the 12.

Messenger: They can't call him one of the 12. He didn't accept that place.

Was he therefore a God outside the 12. When he disagreed, he was no longer one of the 12?

Messenger: Who said he was one of the 12 before that?

My understanding was that you did.

Messenger: I did not say that he was one of the 12 like we have today. 50,000 years ago when this took place, he

SHABAZZ, THE SCIENTIST IN PERSPECTIVE

disagreed with the scientist at that time. Since he disagreed with the Scientist of that time, he cannot be considered one of the roots of the 12. I have said he was I'll admit that, but I am going to go back after (clarify) myself.

I said he was one of the 12, because it was natural for the 12 to have had the power to let him come to naught if he didn't agree with them. But actually at the root of the 12, I don't have a history that puts him in the root of the 12, because these fellows always know what is what and if you are around there as a corrupted root, 50,000 years from now, they would know it.

Sometimes, Brother Minister, when you are talking with me and discussing the roots of the scientist back long ago - the devil calls his pre-historic - (I don't use it), we had ours. It meant the time when he didn't know how to write history. We always have known how to write history. We always have known how to made history. Therefore there never was no pre-history with us. Pre-history puts you in a time like when you were before Our Saviour had arrived - a little silly;

whereas, you don't know actual education, actions or practices to be classified as history or in history. [15]

---

[15] Table Talks of Muhammad, Audio, Date Unknown.

ORIGINAL TRIBE FROM SPIRIT OR PHYSICAL MAN?

Now, He begets not nor is He begotten, this is the theme. When was He not begotten? When had He not beget nor begotten? What do you mean, 'He begets not nor is He begotten? Is He one who does not beget Civilization when He is out of Civilization? Is He one that was not begotten by Civilization and that now the proof is He was not begotten Himself? You see this goes into a very deep science. This is what I whipped one of the Ahmadiyyah Muslims with. He used to be over here on 46th and Wabash (Chicago) at that time. We had what you might call a showdown. He wanted a showdown with me when we were on 43rd Street, so I gave it to him one Monday.

This was his subject that he picked and it also was my subject. We both had the same subject: "Say He (Allah) is One. Allah is He of Whom nothing is independent. He begets not nor is He begotten." The main question in it, with which he was trying to condemn me, was where it says, "and there is none like Him". Well, I knew this would probably be the only thing in the Qur'an he would contend with me [with], that Allah was not man, and I was proving that God was man. I showed him up by proving he didn't understand what he had taken for his defense [and] how it didn't defend him when he was trying to make it serve something other than a man.

I started off with him on the actual noun and pronoun that was used there; that it applies to "something" and not to "nothing." A spirit can't be a noun and a pronoun [and] is not something [in and] of itself. It is something that is emitted by something. You don't have steam coming out of the kettle all by itself. You've got to have something in that kettle for it to be producing steam. The steam is the energy of what you have in there. Well, anyway I won; I can tell you that.

He came down with about 7 or 8 volumes of books. I had one book, the Qur'an. I

ORIGINAL TRIBE FROM SPIRIT OR PHYSICAL MAN?

never did let him get away from the one book. I held him there, because the Qur'an is the chief of all the other books. He and I wrestled there and we had a temple full. It was really something to see how the wisdom of Allah, as taught to me, stands up against anything you can go out there and scrape up brother. What made him so dissatisfied and confused was [that] this was their book. So, he jumped in there and told me not to dispute it from the beginning. He said, "This Qur'an, every Muslim on the earth believes it. If you don't believe in THIS Qur'an, no Muslim in Asia or any place else will like you."

I said, well I would be the same if I were them. I said, if they didn't like this Qur'an, I wouldn't like them. And he was surprised, because he thought I was going to argue the Qur'an as an untrue book. Then I said, here the Qur'an comes after the Bible and not before the Bible. It is a book produced after the Bible and given to Muhammad, but it is a book that verifies the truth of the Bible and the truth of the Bible verifies the truth of the Qur'an and it teaches you that. This he did not try to condemn. He said, "that's right, absolutely true." I said, but we must understand it. And the Bible teaches the same, we must understand. Therefore, the Holy Qur'an is not a book made whereby the average reader can read and understand it; he has to learn what it means. If he did then the prayer for an interpreter from Abraham and Ishmael would not have been made.

The Holy Qur'an often mentions the disbeliever as not understanding. I said, what we call the creed there, "Say He Allah is One God," that's right. I said in the very beginning, He was One. He was before all and from Him we all came, right? He said, "yes!" I said, alright then, that is final and that is conclusive that we must believe that, because we all didn't come at once. 'Say He is One God and there is no God but Him." I said, this I agree 1000%.

I said, but now, He comes here and He says. "Allah is One, He begets not nor is He begotten." I said, but this can't go now back to that one in the beginning, because if that were so, how did we get here if He didn't produce us? He was not begotten, but now we're here from His

ORIGINAL TRIBE FROM SPIRIT OR PHYSICAL MAN?

creation. He created us. Well, if we were created by Him, we are begotten of Him. He gave birth to us. I said, but brother, you have to understand what this is referring to. We couldn't use this as saying He begets not nor is He begotten. We can say He is not begotten, because He was the first and if He was the first, we cannot refer to Him as being begotten for if we did, then we would have to say that one who begot Him would be the God.

So, in that sense, the "He begets not nor is He begotten" is true, but the Qur'an is a book made to [also] condemn the Trinity of Gods and this is what it is referring to. We are to get away from believing Christian beliefs and interpretations of the God. They say there are three Gods. Well, I say if there are three, then here is a begetting and a begotten and we must make a distinction. Who was the first one? The Christians make the three equal, so now, the Qur'an has to shed the light of truth on the God, that the God is not three Gods, but is only One God and He has in the Qur'an here, He is not a Begetter. This is [referring] to the Trinity making

Gods begetting God here, you see? Therefore, this must be stamped out along with the worship of a trinity of Gods.

Our god is referred to throughout the Holy Qur'an as being One God. Your Lord is One Lord it says: "Your Lord is One God." This is to condemn the teaching of that in which the showdown of truth has come; that is, a world that is teaching that the God is three. Here now, I'm saying to you that God is only One God. He is not three. He doesn't beget nor is He begotten.

You say (the Christians) that He begot Jesus for a Son. He didn't do that. The power is in the Jesus to beget, if you understand it rightly.[16]

---

[16] Table Talks of Muhammad, December, 1972.

THE TRIBE OF SHABAZZ IN EAST ASIA (AFRICA)

This particular Tribe of Shabazz was a great people 50,000 years ago. He was our father. Other tribes or families have been produced since that time and have spread out over the earth. Don't get me wrong now, and don't make a mistake in thinking that I am telling you this was the beginning of the man on earth 50,000 years ago. [It would be] like telling you that 30 days ago or 10 days ago or 5 days ago is [our age in comparison] to the age of the Universe. We have no exact record of it, but it runs way into the trillions [of years]. He [Allah, Master Fard Muhammad] took me back around 76 trillion years of the Universe.[17]

---

[17] Tribe of Shabazz, Audio, 1962

THE GOD TRIBE OF SHABAZZ

JOHN HAWKINS AND THE MAKING OF A SLAVE

The John Hawkins history is the history of the enslavement of the seed of Abraham, the Tribe of Shabazz in 1555.
Under the ruler of England, all of the leaders and scholars had come together to map out the drawing up of the 100-year-plan. Sir John Hawkins, a much traveled seaman and trader was among those present.

The problem at hand was the building up of the wilderness of North America. At this time all of Europe was over-populated and being the poorest part of our planet, this continent could not provide for the greedy nature of the white-devils; therefore, they were allowed (by Allah) to expand by the discovery (locating of America, by Columbus in 1492). The problem now was to make America productive in order to send the wealth back to Europe.

THE GOD TRIBE OF SHABAZZ

The blue-eyed devil tried first to enslave the Original members of the Black nation that were over here (Indians or Redman) but the Red man was rebellious and would not submit to being enslaved. This led to war between the two nations, (Red and white).

The devils with their savage ways were able to kill of the Red nation. Out of the many millions of Indians in this country, the devils spared only a few. These were placed on reservations in certain areas of the United States and forced by this wicked government to live in miserable conditions and poverty.

The few remaining of our poor, destroyed Red brothers stand as a mockery conquest to the Black nation and reminder to the white people of today of the great conquering power their forefathers (white devils).

The Red man on this continent are our brothers from the East. They [were driven] away from civilization about 16,000 years ago and were living in exile on this part of the planet earth (now called America and supposedly named

JOHN HAWKINS AND THE MAKING OF A SLAVE

after a devil, a devil named America Vespucci, 1451-1512; he was an adventurer and explorer.

Since the Indians would not submit to slavery, it was asked at the meeting if anyone knew of a people who could be brought to America, and would submit. Sir John Hawkins said, "Yes, there is such a people, they are the greatest nation on the planet earth; the strongest, the wisest and most submissive, but they have never been told a lie; they are the people now living in the rich Nile Valley of Egypt."

Having lived and traded with the Original nation, Sir John Hawkins was given the job of kidnapping Allah's most righteous tribe, stripping them of their knowledge and delivering them to a shameful yoke, he did his job.

Sir John Hawkins sailed to the Egyptian coast in the "Good Ship Jesus", and flying a red flag (it stands for freedom). As he had the wisdom, knowledge, and understanding, which enabled him to act like Original people (Muslims) and not act shameful (evil and wicked). He was, therefore allowed to live among the Holy Tribe of Shabazz (us) who were righteous Muslims at that time. We now are called Negroes, taken from the Latin "Negro" and Greek "Nekros", which means something dead or dead body. We were at that time (prior to 1555) living a highly civilized life along the rich and fertile Nile, submissive to Allah. We were successful and had mastered many of the sciences of life, such as Mathematics, Physiology, Astronomy and many, many others.

Higher mathematics was taught to children and they could be seen playing with diamonds larger than rocks; our wealth was very great.

Sir John Hawkins lived among our people for 29 1/2 years before he committed the evil act in 1555, which doomed the white race to destruction. In all that time, he never told a lie to the holy tribe of Shabazz and he won their confidence. He observed the Black people very closely, learning their nature, habits and science of life. When John Hawkins thought he won the Original nations confidence to the point where

JOHN HAWKINS AND THE MAKING OF A SLAVE

they would believe what he said on face (white) value, he then put his plan into effect. He started a rumor that," there is a land flowing with milk and honey (wealth) across the seas". (America turned out to be such a place for the white devils). This rumor spread until many of the brothers had become curious and wanted to know where this land was (at).

John Hawkins waited until the right moment and then invited the brothers who were interested to come aboard his ship and together they could go over the maps. Once aboard, the Muslims were taken into the hole of the ship where the maps were supposed to be located. When the Muslims were down and out of sight, the crewmen quietly lifted the anchor so that the ship would be carried out to open sea. Upon discovering that they had been tricked and there was no such "Land of milk and honey," the Muslim brothers tried to scramble out of the hole and get off the ship, but they were subdued. John Hawkins set sail for America with his cargo. On the way over, there were some stops for re-supplying the ship with provisions;

anytime one of the Muslims (now so-called Negroes) were allowed out of the hole, he saw it as a chance to escape, many brothers did and having wisdom, knowledge and understanding, were able to build civilizations, such as the civilizations in many Islands of the West Indies.

After traveling from the Holy land, "The good ship Jesus," landed at Jamestown Virginia in 1555. At first the Muslims brothers (our Fathers) were not treated too badly (although they could not return to their own land) because the devils wanted the Black brothers to reproduce themselves (have children) so that he could start "Making" his slave race.

Whenever a child was born to the captured Muslims it was taken away from the Black mother and father. A white (devil) nurse was on hand to take the child to another part of the area to take care of it. The devils (white race) knew that if the Black mother and father were allowed to rear (raise) their own child, they would teach the child knowledge of self and God, and therefore, with such knowledge the child, like his

JOHN HAWKINS AND THE MAKING OF A SLAVE

father before him, would not submit to being a slave (not willingly, anyway).
By using a white nurse, the child would only be taught what the slave-master wanted him to know (no knowledge of self). When one of the Black children would cry for his mother's breast, the devil (white race) nurse would dip a strip of swine fat in molasses and give it to the child to suck on.

The foul piece of nourishment came to be called a "sugar tit". In addition, this evil skunk nurse (white) used to take fat pieces of hog meat and rub it into the poor Black child's head until blood would be popping out. All of these evil acts and dealings with the swine was to ossify (freeze or harden) the brains cells of the black child. This would prevent the Black child from thinking [anything] concerning self. If the Black child (as he grew) would ever question the nurse concerning self, she had been instructed by the slave-master (blue eyed devil) to teach and make the child believe that he was an inferior person [and] created for it.

THE GOD TRIBE OF SHABAZZ

This child grew up to believe, after 64-years of such training and teaching (from 1555 to 1619) the white devils had completed their job of changing the Original Asiatic Blackman (Muslims) to a slave-people.

There stood forth, from a proud righteous and wise people, a mentally blind, deaf and dumb, walking dead man. The devils came together and said, "now that we have completed the making of a slave race, what shall we call them?" The devils (white man) decided upon the name "Negro," which is derived from the Latin word "Necro," and the Greek word "Nekros" which means dead or dealing with the dead. They knew this term fit their made product very well.

The so-called Negro, (mentally dead) were distributed all over America for the purpose of building and making America a strong, productive and powerful country (for the devils) in as short a period as possible.

The year (310) that the Asiatic Blackman spent under slavery in America, is a history of the worst and most inhuman

JOHN HAWKINS AND THE MAKING OF A SLAVE

treatment that any race of people have ever experience, at the hands of this merciless race of devils.

The Blackman was made to suffer every evil injustice a wicked-mind can think of. Some of the acts committed by this evil race against our people for over 300 years, are so filthy and sadistic that they cannot be put into words.

Torture and murder were common-place affairs. For example; A Blackman was made to watch helplessly as the devils took his pregnant woman before all the other Black people, stripped her naked, and with a sharp knife cut her belly open and let the unborn baby fall to the ground. The Black woman would be left screaming for hours on end until death overtook her.

The Black slaves (called Negroes) were made to watch this, thus putting fear into their very nature (all knew something could happen to them).

The Black people were made to eat out of troughs like live-stock. It was nothing to see a devil urinate or otherwise relieve themselves in the troughs that the slaves had to eat out of. No family life was allowed to exist between the Black people. Our blood was crossed up. Fathers were forced to breed with daughters and sons were made to impregnate their sisters or mothers.

The devils themselves would impregnate the Black women (sometimes their own daughters) and put the offspring (their own children) on the block to be sold as slaves. This act alone prove them to be a race of white devils and completely void of love and affection; haters of everything possessing Black blood (even their own children).

Under such treatment the Blackman was made to turn America from wild-land, into a strong and productive nation.
When it became necessary, the wickedly-wise decided it was best to physically free the so-called Negroes, give them a form of education and further use them to advance the prosperity of America. All of the devils did not agree that the Black slaves should be physically freed. This disagreement led to the civil war. At the end of this war, the Blackman was

JOHN HAWKINS AND THE MAKING OF A SLAVE

physically freed, but he was not provided with any land to produce his own needs. Therefore, he had to return to work for the former slave-master in order to survive. Although free, the Blackman was still not independent. Many brothers became irresponsible wanderers.[18]

The Black man here in America has not known anything about his history beyond 400 years ago. 400 years ago he was brought here by the Whiteman and deprived of any knowledge beyond that particular time. He did not teach our people anything about their previous history, [not] even [history] about what we were in the 7th, 8th, 9th, 10th and 11th centuries. He didn't teach us that, because those slave masters were hundred percent together on depriving the slave of any greatness of his history. They absolutely left off all his history up until his entrance into slavery; [consequently, the only] history we have [is] that from the beginning of our fathers being put into slavery. They suffered 300 long years under the hard task

---

[18] Greatest Story Ever Told-History of Sir John Hawkins

masters, murders, lynchers and burners of our people's lives and flesh. This happened just 400 years ago. According to the history of our God, they were brought here around [the year] 1555 and if we subtract 1555 from 1962, we have about 407 years. If we were brought here (and we were) according to the word of God, who is the best knower, who keeps a record of all men and all the actions of men, then today we have been in the Western Hemisphere 407 years to be exact. Without a true knowledge of what went on [prior] to those 407 years, because we take for our knowledge of that time from what the white slave masters wrote, [then] if they were [as] good in trying to hide truth as they are today, we can't tell whether we have a true history of ourselves or not. [We've] had to take what they said.

We were put into servitude slavery and we served something like 310 years. I don't know where these fellows get this stuff about 246 years over here. I don't know where they get that from, but I'm with God and the scientist who gave [put the history] around 400 years here in slavery. [Based on the] actions or events

JOHN HAWKINS AND THE MAKING OF A SLAVE

that are now taking place, which corresponds with the prophesy of Abraham; [whereas, we would] sojourn in strange land that is now ours and [we would] serve a strange people for 400 years. After that time the Lord God would judge that nation and bring [out] again that seed, as [they] are called in the Bible, the people of Abraham, again into their own land and will give them that land and put them over the whole entire earth. According to the Bible, in words, [it told Abraham to] look East, West, North and South and as far as you can see. This will be theirs. [Also] to look at the canopy [over their heads] and if you can number the stars, there then you can count the lost and found people of God, who will return to this land and that they will be multiplied without numbers. [It is also prophesied] that if you go to the sea shore and count the grains of sand on the sea shore you would get [some idea] of what the population of that lost and found you that I shall go after and bring again after they have served 400 years. [They would] serve strangers and would not have any justice in this land. The people will make slaves out of them. They will be ill treated for the full 400 years and I will go and judge that people; for I, in words to say, will avenge them of that people and I will bring them [out] again and plant them in the land.

This is very good to understand and to know, especially my people here in America. We are saying that we are talking on the history of the Blackman in America, as given by Almighty God, Allah, in the person of Master Fard Muhammad. It is up to you [who are reading] to judge whether or not this corresponds with the knowledge of history that you have. With [respect to] prophesy and the scripture, you must forget about Israel being the people who the Bible refers to.

ABRAHAM IS NOT YOUR FATHER

By no means could this be the people of Abraham. Israel is not the people of Abraham. Israel was not a Jew. Israel was not a Christian. Abraham was [neither] a Jew nor a Christian and the Holy Qur'an teaches us that. If you study Abraham's history, you could easily see and understand that he was [neither] a Jew nor was he a Christian, because Christianity had not been organized in Abraham's time. Christianity was just organized after the death of Jesus; therefore, [as] Abraham lived even before Moses, then it could not be his religion (Christianity) nor could he be a Jew, [because] there were no Jews in Abraham time. There were white people, but there were no Jews. The whole entire race of white people were bound in what is known today as Europe. They were there in the hills and cave sides of Europe, not making any history for themselves, until the birth of Moses. The white races' history began with Moses. They count or they record their history from his time. They have very scant knowledge of anything like a history of their own before the birth of Moses and that is through what Moses taught them and what other scientists who knew the history of the white man has taught them.

We today in America should be happy to know that God has visited us and revealed the knowledge of the history of the people of earth today. We have it and it's clear as a crystal if you understand, but you don't understand; therefore, he has chosen me and gave me the understanding to give to you my beloved people. You really need it and it is your salvation. I hope you will benefit from it and will gladly lift up your voice and praise to Allah for giving us the truth today and get away from that slavery worshiping of devils that you are now doing. Without knowledge, you are absolutely worshiping devils and don't know it.

This knowledge has come to you [so] you may direct your face, as the Holy Quran teaches us in the 30th [chapter and the 30th verse] to set your face upright for a

ABRAHAM IS NOT YOUR FATHER

religion, in a right state, a religion that by nature you were created in. It is not a religion in which you cannot obey or cannot believe and practice. It's a religion according to the very nature in which you're born. It is not hard to carry into practice the principles of this religion - it's easy. You don't go through a lot of rituals to get into Islam; in fact, [for] the original people of America - the black man - it is so easy to tell him the 5 principles of this religion and [practice] them, that he almost would think that you have not taught him enough and he will be asking you for more understanding of Islam. That is very easy: just believe in Almighty God, Allah, and believe in His prophets, believe in the scriptures they brought and believe in the resurrection and the judgment of the world; it's easy to believe. It's easy to understand. Want to know what is for the believer to practice? There is much that he should practice, but there are two that are always mentioned; that is, keeping up prayer and paying the poor rate, which means giving in charity to the truth of this religion and your fellow man. This is very easy to understand.

THE GOD TRIBE OF SHABAZZ

BEING ASHAMED OF SALVATION

[We should praise Allah much and teach our children and our children's children to do the same] for this great truth, for this glory that He has shed upon you and I. [We should also be grateful] for this salvation that He has brought to you and I, who were under the shackles of slavery and living in the house of bondage, serving a people who had no love for our fathers and that actually killed them for the fun of it and worked them to death for the fun of it. [They] actually mocked them and taught them in [such] a way to be a mockery for their civilization and for all civilized people of the earth. This is the training of the so-called Negro under slavery in this house of bondage.

You and I should be happy and not be ashamed. So many of you who have so little knowledge of the actual presence of God among you and the wisdom that He's giving you, that you feel ashamed to even to confess His name. As it is written, you feel even ashamed to say that you belong to the Islamic world, which means a Nation of entire submission to the will of God. You are ashamed to even say that you are a Muslim, which means a righteous person. Muslim is something you should be glad to represent yourself as being; yet, you are ashamed because the devil has made you like that: to not to confess that you are a follower of the God of truth and justice.

[The devil makes you feel that] you are not to say that you are a Muslim, [and that] you are not to say you believes in Islam [just] to get their friendship; whereas, for 300-400 years, up until this very hour, regardless of what you accepted and believed in, you accepted whatever they offered you for 400 years. You believed in it and you loved them and you tell them you love them; [consequently], you hate yourself because of this deprived knowledge of self by them. You even hate yourself and you love them [and as a result], you feel ashamed to say you like anything other than what they teach [or to even] say that you are with your own people. I was

BEING ASHAMED OF SALVATION

talking with a Minister one day and he said, "I love everybody; I love white folks." I said yes; there are no people on the earth that actually love their enemies [except] the foolish so- called American Negroes. [This] is due to the lack of knowledge. He has no knowledge of himself or anyone else; therefore, he says a lots of things; [whereas], sometimes he actually lies. He actually lies sometimes in claiming that he loves everybody. If he says that he loves his slave-master, sometime he lies there. He doesn't love his slave-master, but he's afraid of his slave master. He doesn't have the knowledge of himself, his God or the people of God. He knows nothing about it. He knows nothing about the power of God. He knows nothing about anyone, but his slave-master and his children. He knows that they do not treat him as an equal human being. He knows that he doesn't expect justice when he goes into their court. He knows that he's [slave-master] is not going to treat him right if they even stop him on the high way to pretend that he's speeding. Even if he is speeding, he doesn't expect justice. He knows that. Especially in the South if he turns his back, he's likely to be shot after being falsely accused of speeding. He's likely to be shot in the back when he turns his back on the highway patrol officer.

THE PROPHESY OF ABRAHAM

This is a land wherein we just don't have no justice and no friends; yet, this is the land that Abraham said God revealed the history or the revelation [of] concerning his people being lost for 400 years. This particular spot where we are was not known to the scientists, [or] where this place would be. All they had was that they would be lost somewhere on the earth, but just where it was, they didn't know. At that time of the revelation to Abraham, you must remember that the Red Indians were in this part of our earth.

East, West & Red Indians

[They] had been brought over here in the Western Hemisphere, according the revelation of Allah to me, in the person of Master W.D Fard Muhammad, to whom praises be forever. They had been here for 16,000 years, [after being] driven out of what is known today as East Indian. [The] country that now borders Pakistan. [They] once were the masters of that entire country. They are called the East Indians to distinguish them from the West Indians, but the Red Indian is the brother of those in Indian today and if you look at them, you will soon see that they are brothers by their features.

All of this is to give to you the knowledge of self, but our fathers were brought here just 400 years ago and have withstood more evil treatment than any human being at the hand and mouth of another, since man has been on the face of the earth. You say, "No, no, you are wrong." I say, "Yes, yes, I'm right," and I will make you prove that I'm wrong.

If you have any history; wherein, any other people [have] ever suffered at the hands of a human being or human beings [more] ruthlessly and mercilessly as we have suffered at the hands of white America, I will submit, bow to you, and I will pay for the lie and be willing to suffer anything that may satisfy your desire as being the price that I should pay, even if It's death.

We don't have [any] history back in the last 4,000 years that equals the cruel

THE PROPHESY OF ABRAHAM

history that the so-called Negroes have suffered in America; we don't have anything like that. You say, "Well the Jews." I even hear the white people say sometimes, when this evil treatment they have given to us under slavery for the last 400 years, that there was slavery among all people. "We all have suffered slavery." Today, some of our own scholars, of our own color, are now using the same terms [of reference]. [It's] now very common to see them take up anything [mimics what] the white man use to throw at us to see [if] whether or not he can get away with deceiving us in some false statement. [For this] the scholars of our people should be ashamed of themselves for taking up the same slang or [buzz words] of mockery used on us, since they are our brothers and have suffered the same treatment that we have suffered, and if not, what their fathers have suffered. Why should you take sides with people who you known all your life to have been an enemy of the black man here in America, and help him to make mock of your own people, or help him to claim that he's justified in saying this or doing this to you and I. This is very shameful and wicked on the part of the intellectual, scholars and scientists people of our kind in America, who are ashamed to confess their own. They want to be like their slave masters' children; therefore, they deny and reject any glory coming to their own kind.

Pretty soon Allah will change this particular thinking; I'm assured of that. It is written and prophesied that every one of my people will be resurrected into the knowledge of their own and they all will go to their God, go to their people and go to their own country. They all will be happy and they all will live in peace. They all will praise and glorify the God who delivered them. As one place here in the Bible says, that in that day and time they shall no more say the God who brought them up out of the land of Egypt, but the God who searched the earth and found them, gathered them together and brought them back to their own country. [They will speak] not of a God that went into Egypt and got a handful of people, but a God that went after a nation.

A LOST AND FOUND NATION

We find He refers to us as a nation. If we don't consider ourselves as a nation today, take for an [example] that there are many people called a nation who got their independence, some of whom didn't have over a million and a half in their population and some didn't have over 5 million, but they are called a nation; yet, we number 20 million. If 20 million don't think that they are a nation, I say, when will you recognize yourself as a nation? You cannot be respected as a nation at the present time, because you are swallowed up in the government of America and there is no sign of you on the outside. [This is] because of your name and your way of life that you live, which is trying to imitate the white man; therefore, it doesn't look like you even exist. To look at you from the outside [world], you are little Jones slave boy of the master Jones. Observing from the outside, no one can tell whether or not little Jones is white or big Jones is white or both are white or whether there is black anywhere in America until they come among you.

Going in the name of the white man for 310 years up until the coming of Almighty God Allah, in the person of Master Fard Muhammad to Whom be praised forever. [Our people] had no knowledge of our strain and had no knowledge of the whereabouts. It was 60 years of searching before we were discovered here in America, but we had been found. You don't have to be frightened and you don't have to wander without a name. You have been found and you are no more termed lost or forsaken. You have a God on your side today. It is written in the book of Ezekiel, "Even I will go and search for them. I will bring them again and I will plant them upon the mountain of Israel. They shall lie down in peace and none shall make them afraid. I will bless them with peace like rivers of water. I will not forsake them. I will visit them;" your Bible teaches you all of this. The Holy Qur'an refers to you time and again; [wherein it says] that He will give you life. He will put you on top and plant you in the place where another will be removed.

A LOST AND FOUND NATION

This has been the course of history among man every since we had history.

Every time that one disobeys Almighty God that ruler is put down and once every 25,000 years we takes a new start according to the word of Almighty God up until this present day we use that particular number of years that brought about a change in our history. Every 25,000 years there came about a total change. Almighty God Allah said that once upon an time they wrote history for 35,000 years. We are the writers He says, meaning the darker people of the earth who has been here ever since the universe was created or the one that actually record history of everything that takes place on the planet earth and the one who knows what have happened and what will happen it is our own people. Wouldn't you rather have been a member of people like that? [Only] if you can be made to believe. I'm satisfied that you will be as happy as I am and my followers if you can believe that this is the truth and it is the truth beyond a shadow of a doubt it's nothing but the truth. We knows about the 6,000 years which means or doesn't mean anymore to we now that has been taught 60,000 years, 60 trillion years ago, this 6,000 years old history of the Caucasian race seems like talking about here just yesterday because of the long, long, long history that we has been taken over.

THE LAKE OF FIRE

Here in Chicago where so much fine wisdom of God and the religion of Islam has been pour into the Chicago original dark people for the last 25 or 30 years, now you are the one that is still slow to respond. It is a shame for Detroit and Chicago to be lagging behind other cities which is now increasing in converts throughout the nation from the Atlantic to the West Coast and from the border of Canada to the Gulf we find our people today as Ezekiel describes them under the symbol of dry bones.[19]

---

[19] Tribe of Shabazz, Audio, 1962

THE GOD TRIBE OF SHABAZZ

Think over how much you have been preached to like Jerusalem.

The Jesus said he did all that work in Jerusalem, and that , even if Sodom and Gomorrah had had that kind of wonk they would have believed and repented long ago. I say the same thing about Chicago and Detroit: For 40 years I have taught the people of these two cities enough for them to walk into Heaven. Regardless to how high it is or how wide it is, they should be able to walk in it, because they have been taught everything. They should be scientists at the Knowledge of Truth.

But just think over the prophecy. When the time came the people still were in doubt and it overtook them at a time they knew not. This is Truth.

That is the way it was with Noah and Lot. When the time came, they didn't have anybody; so, he had to turn them all over to destruction. Think over the hundreds of thousands of our people in Chicago to be turned over to destruction. If you are not a believer, you won't go anyplace but to that [destruction].

THE LAKE OF FIRE

Don't think I am going to try to defend you and you are at home asleep instead of at the Temple. I am the One.

I have said that I am the One who will be here to do this kind of work. You will say [the same things], like the disbelievers said to the prophets in those days. They begged the prophets to let them go along with them, but they weren't worthy. Look at all of the converts Lot thought he had.

The Angels kept telling him they would cut the number down if he could bring it up. He kept running back thinking that he had more followers than that five or ten or fifteen. He thought he could get that before he would get out of the door, but he was not able to do it. He just was able to bring before the Angels four or five.

The Bible and the Holy Qur'an speak of a very small number coming from you out of millions. The Bible says two out of a family and then it says in another place that the people would be very small in number that believe; and it looks like that.

What's holding you back? "Oh, I don't believe nothing is going to take place like what he's talking about. He may be talking just for money." Well, if we are, your money would not be any good if these things come to pass and they are going to come to pass.

A Man like Me who has been wrestling with your disbelief for years gets disgusted sometimes.

We are having some bad, bad, bad troubles in this part of the world as you read and as you hear over the radio. There is suffering. Don't think you are immune to it. The Holy Qur'an says you will hear it coming from a distant place with its Vehemence raging and roaring. It is on [the] way to hit Chicago. It will frighten you nearly to death when you see these things going on in America and in Chicago.

Chicago and many other cities of America will be treated like these that you are reading about and listening to. That same kind of trouble, or worse, will come here. I am like Jesus said after he

THE LAKE OF FIRE

had taught Jerusalem so long and so hard. He was disgusted. He got outside and looked back at her: "Oh Jerusalem, Jerusalem, that killeth the prophets and stoned them that are sent unto thee. How often would I have covered thee as a mom covers her little chicks with her wings. I only say if thou wouldst believe, but thou now art left desolate. There will be no more prophets after me. I was your last one. Woe to Jerusalem. You hate prophets. You don't like them." That is an awful pitiful crime. In about 70 years another king came in and sacked the city taking away the independence of the Jews. These things will soon come to America.

Then what will you who are depending on the devil Caucasian here do? You won't have anything to look forward to. Some of you are loving the devil Caucasian so well and so sincerely that you don't want to hear me call him a devil. But you just stick around, [those of you] who are loving him. He and you both will be pushed into the lake of fire together.

"And I saw," saith the Revelations, "the devil and those who follow him pushed into a lake of fire and brimstone." Don't think these people are lying just to frighten you into believing. No. It is coming to pass. Prophets don't lie. The people call them liars but they don't lie.

The Sun is going down in the West. This Teaching will raise a powerful Sun of Truth from this part of our planet by Me Who Allah (God) raised up among you. No more will you look towards the East after this for the Light of Truth to come.

The Light of Truth, which the scientist of the East were not able to give you will come from the West.[20]

---

[20] The Lake of Fire, Article By Elijah Muhammad, Date unknown

THE NEW QIBLAH

[A lot of Believers don't realize that in 1972, at the lecture given at the Opening Day of the New Temple No. 2 in Chicago, Messenger Elijah Muhammad stopped us from facing the East when we pray.]

Messenger Elijah Muhammad's words from that lecture were published in the C issue of Muhammad Speaks Newspaper. The Messenger said: "We have to build a new world. As you noticed while the Minister was praying, I had not my face turned towards the East, for the sunlight of truth is not to come from the East; it is to come from the West! And since God, Almighty, In the Person of Master Fard Muhammad, Has Made me the first to rise from you, I must turn you on a light coming from here--from the West. No more shall we turn our face to the East, looking for light from the East, for the Sun of Light has risen in the West!!!......" (Muhammad Speaks, June 9, 1972)

This world, according to God's teaching to me, was brought about by grafting. The White race are a grafted people who were grafted from the Original people, the dark people. [From the process of grafting the white race], in making them we made a Brown race, Yellow race and Red race, to get to the finality of the germ and at the end there was nothing but White. This is what the Scientist was after. He was after grafting the germ into its last stage: white and blue eyes. No other race has that, because the white man is the end of it. We can't make nothing else. This is what the Holy Qur'an refers to when it says, "We have tried everything and everything obeys Allah but man."

WHY DID ALLAH MAKE DEVIL?

It is often asked by people, why did Allah make devil. It's not a bad question and it's not a bad answer. Many people think that the God that created the heavens and the earth is the same God that created the devil or Satan. We say Satan, because the meaning is better understood. Satan in the Arabic language means a person or persons who is evil and whose evil is not confined to themselves. It's evil affects others and that's what's actually meant when we say Satan. Satan is person that's evil and their evil affects others.

The Whiteman is not a descendant of Satan. We didn't have a Satan before the Whiteman. The Whiteman is Satan himself. He is not a descendant of something; he is what he is in his own sphere or nation. He is not a descendant. The God that [made] the Whiteman [made] him for [the] purpose of showing forth a wisdom that was yet hidden in the God that was not made manifest. This was the main purpose. It was not a useless thing for which the race was made, and it wasn't the God that created the heavens and earth in truth that made Satan. It was a rebel of that God that made this race of people.

The Caucasian race or white people, as they are called, are called Caucasian because of the quality or [description] of the man. He originally is weak bone and stale faced. This is a person with a stale color and their bones are weak and color Caucasian. Actually, he was made white. This was brought about just recently, compared to trillions and billions of years. Their birth is just here of today approximately 6,000 years ago. A Blackman is the Father of the Caucasian race. His name was Yakub. They call him Jacob in English, but in Arabic, it's Yakub.

He didn't make them to attack God as many scholars on the germ or question of devil and Satan desire to [entertain], he was not made exactly for all of that and he [Yakub] didn't have all of that in his mind.

WHY DID ALLAH MAKE DEVIL?

What idea [Yakub] actually had in his mind was to make a man that was just opposite to what we were or a people that was opposite to us in general or an absolutely different person without the nature or ideas like ours, but a new people altogether to try them at ruling. His main idea was to make a people that could rule us and not be us. He, for example, was angry with the God and wanted to attack God and His rule, [per se]. Yakub was not that type of man. He was very wise and one of the Righteous.

The Bible refers to him as being one of the Angels. He lost His place because of what He did. The Bible doesn't give to you a clear picture of it. His fall was not due to attacking God in war, as the Bible teaches, but His idea was wrong; therefore, the Gods did not agree that He makes man in the Holy Land and that if He wanted to make His man they would agree that He makes it, but it must be out of the sphere of the Righteous people since His idea was unrighteous. They exiled Him for having the idea of creating unrighteousness to rule Righteousness. He was so powerful at that time that they were actually afraid to oppose His ideas, because He was too wise a Man. He could have caused a lot of trouble at the time.

The reason this talk is being taken up with you is because we are living in a time when the same thing is in the mind of this people. They would like to destroy the entire human family of the earth if they are destroyed. The war scientists of Russia and America are ready and prepared to destroy each other, but a silent scientist knows what they have prepared and knows they can do so if they were given the freedom, but they will not be given that freedom to destroy all human beings. You can't do it.

There is always one left from that family at the beginning who have the key or holds the key. He holds the key and you can't get the key. What I mean is the key to the knowledge of how to control the power of the nature in which the universe has been created. When you are lucky enough to land that key to control the power of nature, then you can rule. Anyone can rise up as your enemy, because there are no people that can control the power or forces of nature,

WHY DID ALLAH MAKE DEVIL?

but a few. There are only a few. They are secret. You wouldn't know them if you saw them. They have been here all the while. What I mean is that when he [one] dies, he leaves it with his son and his son keeps it. It goes like that.

There is no such thing as the scientist of this world being able to destroy the whole thing though they are able to do it, but they can't do it. This man was able to do it. He drilled a tube into our planet at that time with dynamite material for better than 10,000 miles. He drilled a tube into it like you are mining coal. He went into our planet a couple thousand miles and filled it with high explosives, dynamite. It was not the weak kind used presently. It was 30% percent stronger than what used today. He built it up to the extent that once set off it would end the whole thing. However He missed.

From the explosion, this part that we are on dropped 36,000 miles from its original pocket from which it was rotating. The explosion blasted the other part known as moon, although it has no water, out 12,000 miles away from the original pocket before it turned over and lost the water. Consequently, the earth has the water that was on that part and that makes this part 3/4 covered with water, because it took that part. We use to not have that much water in our atmosphere. At sea level, we have much water, but when the moon and the earth was together we didn't have it.[21]

---

[21] Buzz Anderson Interview, Phoenix, AZ 1964

THE NEW WORLD WON'T ACCEPT THE OLD

This world's time was up, according to word of Allah, it suppose to be the end of this world in 1914. They all knew that - the scientist. The extension of time is due to the resurrection. The resurrection must take place before there can take place of the present world or this way of civilization. We have had, according to the teachings of Almighty Allah, many Gods that have set up worlds in the past and they have had civilizations of this or of that type, but when the next one comes in this is all erased so you won't pattern after the other man. The same goes for this world. When this world is destroyed you won't be able to get nothing from it. Like the Bible teaches you, it will be destroyed and all its works: meaning, everything even the lamps. You will have to make your own lamp. It was for this world and this God. Now you must build from your brain another world. Everything will be different. You are not allowed to pattern after another, because all the markings, signs and libraries will be destroyed. As you today know that according to history, Noah, his people was destroyed. There were a few towns and cities there, but we have no knowledge of their civilization or histories and no more than a word or two here and there. Sodom and Gomorrah was destroyed, but you have no knowledge of their history because there was none saved. Their library was burned up; therefore you can't get any knowledge of how they carried on. Only thing you get is that they were wicked and that's all you know and that they did this kind of wickedness. How they built and what they built from or made this or that, you don't get that.

Will you have some knowledge of what you came from? You will have some knowledge of what you left from for a time, but you will be put in a place where it won't be published. It won't be put in any books. You won't be allowed to speak the language anymore. That also goes for the next life. You won't even speak this language. Every said to you

THE NEW WORLD WON'T ACCEPT THE OLD

will be said in the next language. You won't be allowed to say "lamp" for example. You won't call it after the previous language.[22]

You won't be allowed to speak the language of this world 20 years after you have gone out of it. 20 years from that day you won't be allowed to speak one world of English.[23]

---

[22] Messenger Elijah Muhammad, Audio, Baltimore, MD 1960.
[23] Ibid.

THE GOD TRIBE OF SHABAZZ

THE GREAT BOOK

Today you have the base of the Bible and Holy Qur'an which was taken from that same Great book I mentioned to you that is preserved in the Holy City Mecca. There is no such thing as a prophet getting a scripture or book dropped out of the sky. There never was a book dropped out of the sky to no prophet and don't look for one today, unless you carry it up there and drop it back down. The scripture that we call Bible and Holy Qur'an were already preserved and written thousands of years before it was ever given to a prophet.

15,000 years ago, 24 scientist got together, so God has revealed to me, and 23 of them was ordered by the 24th to write the present Bible and Holy Qur'an that you and I now have. That is not all of that Great book. It's a Great book. It's just little portions of that book that's given to certain prophets for his people and for that time. They are limited. The time is limited for them. All the scripture you have is limited. There is no permanent scripture; it's all limited.

There are permanent records made of them and permanent records will be kept.

After this world or the judgment of this world, this history that you now know will be put away and the public will never read anything of it anymore. If there be civilization for millions or billions of years from now, no common people of that civilization will ever read the history of this world. Why? The answer is this: This world is opposed to the world of Righteousness and the next world is a world of Righteousness; therefore, the next world will forbid any teaching or reading of anything other than Right. [This is necessary because] if you would read of such world and practice the art of this world, you would have this world living into the next world. So, to deprive you of that practice, the God has said to me, that they are going to burn this world and burn all of their literature so you that won't get a hold to any of it in the hereafter to practice; not even to read. He has said to me that He was going to destroy it and not allow you to carry out if you are one of the lucky ones going out. I am not too sure if you

THE GREAT BOOK

are going to be that lucky. If you are a lucky one going out, you won't be able to carry anything but yourself.[24]

Your good ears have been [so] stopped up by falsehood and blindness [when it comes to your salvation] that you might not understand, [so much so that], even on the coming of God Himself [in] the last day that God Himself would find [it] impossible to open your eyes or unstop your deaf ears, [based on how well] sealed [they are] by the slave master and his children. You are living in the time that you must be separated, not integrated. [This is the] time of separation, foolish brother. Don't get the idea that you are not living in no such time. This is the time [of] the resurrection of the dead; this is the judgment. This is the person of God. He is not to come, He has already come. This is the time and end of all the prophets. [If] you read and search the knowledge of scripture, you yourself [will] understand by what you read that this is the end of the prophecy. [It] is true if

---

[24] Messenger Elijah Muhammad, Audio; Baltimore, MD 1960.

you will avail yourself of it. We are living in a great time of trouble of the departure of the two worlds: one is departing from the other and the other is emerging in the departed place of the other.

We will have a new entire government and a new civilization from what you see of the old world. We will not take any pattern from the old world. The God feels Himself too independent to use a pattern from an old world. We have the civilizations of ancient people in the history, but the knowledge of their civilization or how it worked, we don't have any books or text books from their libraries. All were destroyed with that people once every 25,000 years so says Almighty God Allah to me. They destroyed a whole histories of what went on for the past 25,000 years and they make a new one, take a note of that history and put it away and preserves from the masses and the knowledge of the common people and no man is allowed to look in it or read their history except He [that's] going to be a "Wonder" man. [He would be the One Who would know] how to change a civilization or

THE GREAT BOOK

[cause] a universal change. [If a change] is about to take place, he will be the one to bring about a change and that Book is given to Him to read or study to know what happens with us on this planet for the [next] 25,000 years, 50,000 years or a million or a billion or trillion years.

The coming of now Just One we are now becoming acquainted with, we have the knowledge of the very beginning and knows all of the history of the Universe from their creation. There is no end of his knowledge, wisdom and understanding; therefore, you and I are lucky to be here in this time to get some of this knowledge that we are now imparting to you.

We don't have the book that will take us into that great knowledge into the hereafter, because of the presence of this world, but soon after this world, we will have a new book that will take us in the beyond, but at the present time, we are finishing up what is written in the present book or scriptures; mainly the Bible and Holy Quran. With this knowledge up to the door of the hereafter, you and I should understand it so that we will know our place today and where to stand in the departure of the old world and the merging in of the new world.

You are a great nation. You are the members of a mighty nation. You are the members, according to the teachings of Almighty God Allah, of a people that has no beginning nor ending. You are a great and strong people, but you went to sleep and slept for 6,000 years. Now, the whole nation of our kind is rousting themselves to take hold [of] the reigns of civilization and rule once more and again forever.[25]

As-Salaam-Alaikum

Elijah Muhammad
Messenger of Allah

---

[25] Tribe of Shabazz, Audio, 1962.

Catalog Requests

For a comprehensive collection of books, documents, DVDs & Audio CDs, simply write for a free catalog to the address in the front or back of the book.

Printed in Great Britain
by Amazon